STEM!

SCIENCE

EDITED BY
MARZIA TEMPOLI

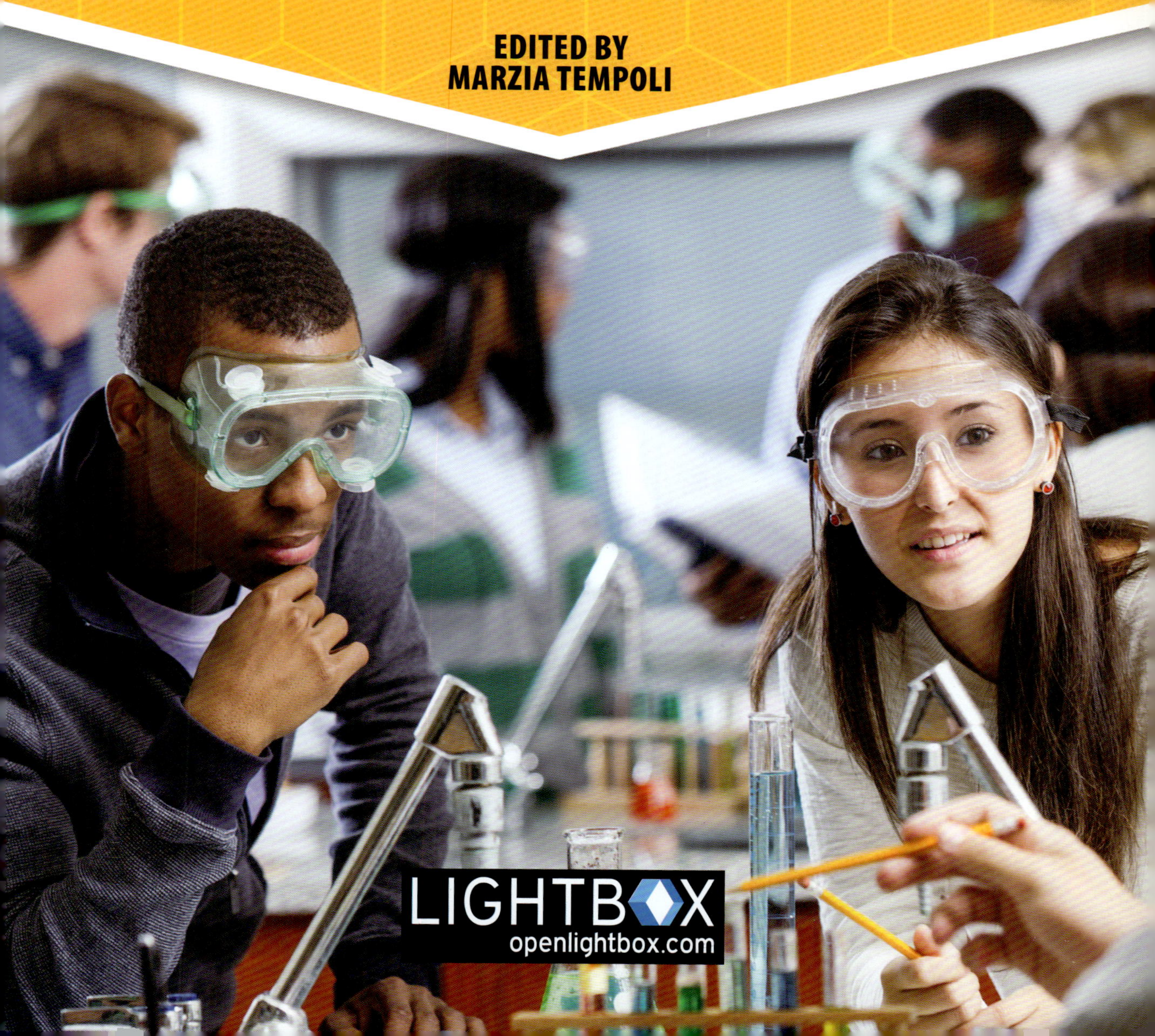

LIGHTBOX
openlightbox.com

LIGHTBOX

Go to
www.openlightbox.com
and enter this book's
unique code.

ACCESS CODE

LBXU9822

Lightbox is an all-inclusive digital solution for the teaching and learning of curriculum topics in an original, groundbreaking way. Lightbox is based on National Curriculum Standards.

STANDARD FEATURES OF LIGHTBOX

AUDIO High-quality narration using text-to-speech system

ACTIVITIES Printable PDFs that can be emailed and graded

SLIDESHOWS Pictorial overviews of key concepts

VIDEOS Embedded high-definition video clips

WEBLINKS Curated links to external, child-safe resources

TRANSPARENCIES Step-by-step layering of maps, diagrams, charts, and timelines

INTERACTIVE MAPS Interactive maps and aerial satellite imagery

QUIZZES Ten multiple choice questions that are automatically graded and emailed for teacher assessment

KEY WORDS Matching key concepts to their definitions

STEM!

SCIENCE

CONTENTS

WHAT IS SCIENCE?

The word "science" comes from the Latin word *scientia*, which means knowledge. There are sometimes said to be three branches of science. These are described as formal science, which is logic and math, social science, which is the study of human society and history, and natural science, which is the study of the physical world. Today, the word "science" is what most people commonly use to describe the natural sciences.

The natural sciences can be divided into three broad branches of study. These are **chemistry**, **physics,** and **biology**. Each of these branches also has subsections. Earth science, for example, is a branch of science that studies Earth and its atmosphere. Earth science includes **geology**, **meteorology** and **oceanography**.

Scientists believe that the universe works according to **laws** and processes. These can be examined and tested. Science in general is about finding out how the world and the universe work.

▲ There are estimated to be about eight million scientists currently active in all branches of scientific research worldwide.

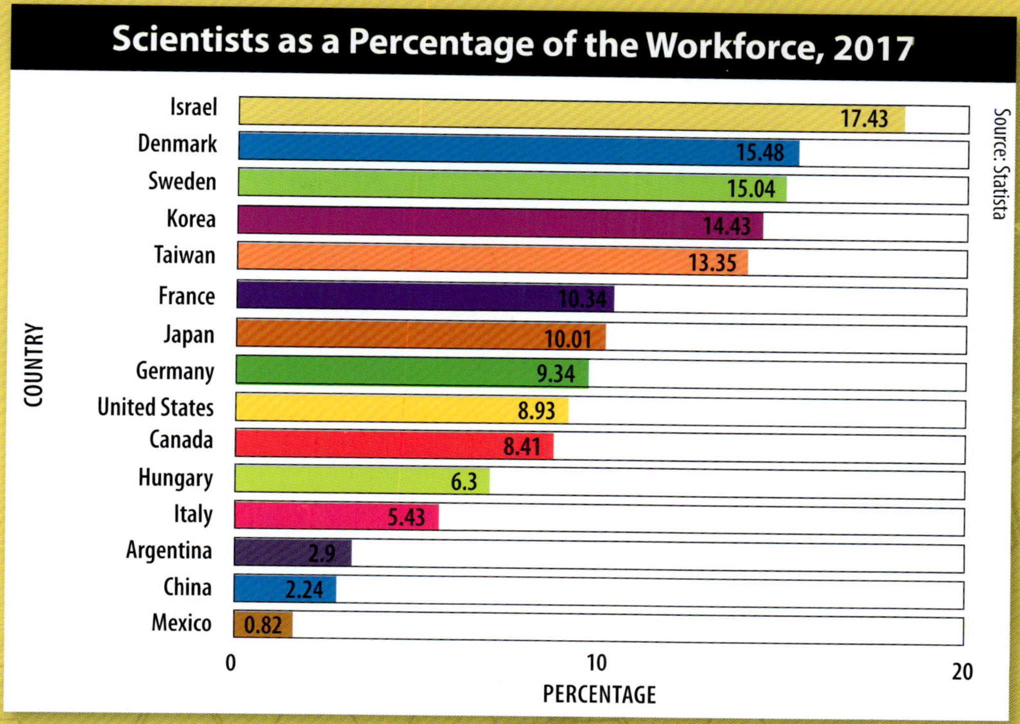

Modern science is studied using strict scientific method. This is a procedure that tests a theory about something. Many theories fail to pass the test. Science involves thinking of reasons why something might happen, and testing that theory by observation, measurement, and experimentation. Using this method, science has enabled people to begin to understand the structure of life on Earth and the history of the universe.

➧ Scientific research has discovered the structure of tiny objects, the enormous size of the universe, and the building blocks of life itself.

SCIENCE WORLDWIDE

People have always looked at the world around them and tried to figure out why things happen. Many ancient peoples thought that unseen gods controlled what happened. Many of the gods in the ancient world were connected to nature. The Norse god Thor was said to cause thunder, lightning, and storms.

People in different parts of the world invented ideas that seemed to explain what they were observing. Almost all these ideas made some sense. Some are still useful today. However, most of them were wrong in some way.

From the 1600s onward, the introduction of scientific method enabled scientists to begin to understand life on Earth, and the enormity of the universe.

Cape Canaveral, Florida, United States
In 1924, U.S. scientist Edwin Hubble was the first person to explain the huge size of the universe. Now, the U.S. space exploration center at Cape Canaveral leads the world in space research. The United States has been at the forefront of astronomy for 100 years.

Giza, Egypt
The ancient Egyptians put into practice precise observations of the sky. Although built in 2560 BC, the Great Pyramid was built to face north-south accurately.

London, Great Britain
The idea of having a clear scientific method was devised in London in the early 1600s by Francis Bacon.

Berlin, Germany
German scientist Lise Meitner described the power of splitting the atom. She and her team discovered this in Berlin during the twentieth century.

Beijing, China
From 250 BC, Chinese scientists thought that substances that appeared to be opposites might actually be similar. This theory of the Yin and the Yang made sense of freezing and boiling.

The Ancient and Medieval World

Most of early science and observation was for practical purposes. People used what knowledge they had to work out the best time to plant crops and when to harvest them. They passed down information on how to make tools from wood, stone, and metal. They also observed the night sky, often for religious purposes.

From about 500 BC, thinkers in Greece had begun to write down what they knew about the world. The philosopher, Aristotle, tried to write down what he had discovered about living things and natural forces. He believed in making detailed observations. He thought there were four **elements**. They were earth, air, fire, and water. The whole world was a made up of these.

Blacksmiths in the ancient world used fire to melt and soften metals. They shaped the metal into objects they could use.

Greek thinking was important in Europe during the period of the Roman Empire, from 27 BC to 476 AD. When the empire collapsed, Islamic scholars built on the discoveries that had been made by the Greeks and Romans. In medieval Europe, all knowledge was believed to come from God. However, a handful of people called **alchemists** tried to take a more scientific approach. Some of their experiments provided useful information. They broke down some **matter** and combined it with other substances. Toward the end of the Middle Ages, people in Europe rediscovered Greek knowledge that had been preserved in the Arab world.

Some medieval experimenters thought that matter could be turned into other substances. They attempted to mix substances together to make gold.

ATOMIC THEORY OF THE UNIVERSE

The Greek philosopher Democritus is believed to have lived from about 460 to about 370 BC. He is said to have visited Egypt to discuss math with Egyptian scholars. Democritus believed that everything in the universe was composed of small, invisible **atoms**. This was called **atomic theory**. Democritus said there were many different types of atoms. Some were strong, some were weak. This idea was taken up by the Roman writer Lucretius centuries later, and then rediscovered in the fifteenth century in Europe.

Democritus believed that there were no limits to time or space. He said the universe was everlasting.

The Early Modern World

Science in Europe began to change in the 1500s. Nicolaus Copernicus described how Earth moves around the Sun. This theory was revolutionary. Before that, people believed that the Sun moved around Earth.

In the early 1600s, the British thinker Francis Bacon carried out scientific experiments on living things and wrote down the results. This was the development of the scientific method. Bacon believed that everything must be tested by observation, or by experiments, and every theory must be proven.

The experiments of the French chemist, Antoine Lavoisier, showed that all matter is made up of a number of elements. Instead of the classical elements of earth, air, fire, and water, he listed 55 chemical elements. This work was the basis of modern chemistry.

In the late 1600s, the English scientist, Isaac Newton, explained that a force called gravity is what makes objects move toward each other. He used this theory to describe what he called the laws of motion. Newton thought that everything is governed by rules, or laws, that can be explained. Newton's ideas inspired other scientific researchers. During the 1700s, Frenchman Antoine Lavoisier discovered that oxygen is necessary in order for things to burn. He also recognized the existence of basic elements. British scientist John Dalton then proposed that all matter is composed of atoms. Swedish chemist Jöns Jacob Berzelius compiled a table of **atomic weights** and invented the **chemical notation** that is still in use today.

GALILEO GALILEI

Galileo Galilei was an Italian astronomer, physicist, and engineer. He had a wide range of scientific interests. He devised a method to measure the flight of a missile through the air and discovered that it followed a curving path called a parabola. In 1642, he discovered that pendulums could be used to regulate mechanical clocks. He also discovered that objects fall to the ground at the same speed, even if they are different sizes. In 1609, Galileo invented a telescope to look at the Moon and the planets. He saw that heavenly objects followed circular orbits. His work made clear his belief that Earth moved around the Sun. This brought him into conflict with the Catholic Church. He was questioned and put under house arrest for the rest of his life.

▲ Using his telescope, Galileo saw objects that had never been seen before.

In the early 1800s, the English scientist Michael Faraday made experiments with magnetism. He found out how to create electricity. His discoveries were the foundation for the development of modern physics. There were also great advances in medicine and biology. The discovery of how the blood circulates around the body had been made by William Harvey in the 1600s. This had inspired further research. The use of microscopes now revealed the existence of the many small living organisms that affect the human body.

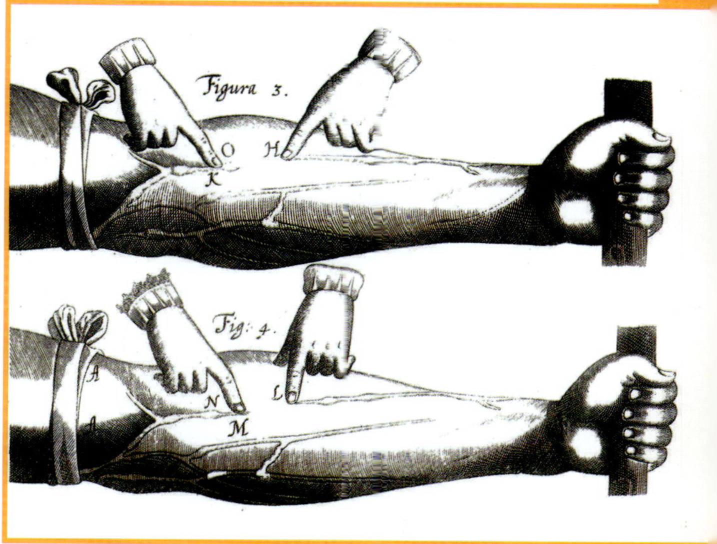

▲ In 1628, William Harvey published a work that included detailed drawings of blood vessels. The book described how blood leaves the heart through the arteries and is returned to the heart through the veins.

Modern Physics

In 1861, Scottish scientist James Clerk Maxwell published *On Physical Lines of Force*. The work became known as the Maxwell equations. His paper proposed that electricity, magnetism, and light are all related. Maxwell's equations described **electromagnetic radiation**.

Over the next 100 years, there was a revolution in physics. First, it was discovered that atoms were not the smallest blocks of matter. When atoms break down they release enormous amounts of energy. Second, came Albert Einstein's theory of relativity. Einstein's idea was that time itself can vary, and that there is a relationship between energy and the amount of matter in an object. Modern physics looks not only at how things work over huge distances and periods of time, but also at very small particles.

The Large Hadron Collider (LHC) in Switzerland is more than 17 miles (27 km) long. It speeds up the movement of particles so they crash into each other and break apart. "Hadron" refers to particles smaller than an atom. It was completed in 2008.

As technology has advanced, physics has had a wider application. Scientists are now able to create temperatures in laboratories that are far colder than before. This has opened up a branch of physics that studies extremes of temperature and the effect they have on substances. The energy of electricity has been used to invent more efficient types of engines. In turn, much of physics has become practical and is closely linked to engineering.

Physicists have also been able to harness light. They have slowed down the light beam. Light has also been used to act as a laser, to cut through objects.

Physicists have been able to use very low temperatures to turn gases into liquids. This has medical applications.

By creating lasers, physicists have invented tools that can be used in medicine as well as in industry.

A 60-watt light bulb emits
180,000,000,000,000,000,000
particles of light per second.

In 2018, scientists made the coldest liquid water yet, at
-50 Fahrenheit
(-45 Celsius).

Light travels at a speed of
186,282 miles per second
(299,792 kilometers per second).

Modern Chemistry

By the end of the 1800s, chemists believed that they had discovered almost all of the elements that had ever existed. They also believed that atoms could not be altered, and were the smallest building blocks of all matter. In 1869, Russian scientist Dmitri Mendeleev constructed a **periodic table**, in which all the elements had a place.

In the years following the publication of Mendeleev's table, however, several other elements were discovered. They paved the way for the science of chemistry as it is known today. The biggest revolution was the discovery of radioactivity. Marie and Pierre Curie found that the atoms of some elements gave off **radiation** and became other elements over a period of time.

During the 1900s, the nature of atoms was understood. Atoms consist of tiny amounts of matter in a nucleus. Electrons carry electricity and orbit around the nucleus.

Marie Curie discovered the elements radium and polonium. In 1911, she won the Nobel Prize in Chemistry for her work.

The work of a chemist involves finding out which elements make up a substance. They also study how that substance reacts with other gases, liquids, or solids.

In the modern world, chemistry has become increasingly important. It has many practical applications. Much of what people use in everyday life, from the gasoline in automobile engines to the packaging used for food has been created by a chemist in a laboratory.

The study of chemical substances and how they interact with each other has also helped to improve the effectiveness of medicines. The science of biochemistry has led to revolutions in the treatment of illnesses and disease.

TYPES OF CHEMISTRY

Chemistry is divided into five fields. Organic chemistry examines substances that contain carbon. Inorganic chemistry deals with reactions and substances that do not involve carbon. Analytical chemistry is the name for a branch of chemistry that aims to separate and identify different substances. Physical chemistry looks at how the theories of physics apply to chemistry. Biochemistry is the study of the molecules that make up all animal and plant life.

Modern Life Science

In the 1800s, British naturalist and biologist Charles Darwin developed a theory of evolution. He believed that all living creatures were descended from other living creatures, and that different species of plant and animal changed gradually over time to adapt to their environment. Change occurred naturally but accidentally.

Darwin's theory was revolutionary. It is the basis of modern life science, although it was widely criticized at the time. The discovery of the structure of the deoxyribonucleic acid (DNA) molecule in the 1950s was equally revolutionary. DNA is the means by which humans inherit characteristics from their parents.

Life scientists who specialize in botany spend much of their time examining how plants grow. They also study how crops can be protected from pests.

In the mid-1800s, Gregor Mendel, from Austria, worked with plants. He discovered that organisms pass on their **genes** in a certain sequence. The discovery of DNA's structure meant that for the first time, scientists could look at the entire genetic code of a person. In the 1900s, new technologies such as magnetic resonance imaging (MRI) scans made it possible to understand the structure of the human brain, and how humans think and feel.

Today, many life scientists study climate change. They also look at the effects of human activity on the environment. They advise governments on actions to stop human pollution of the planet.

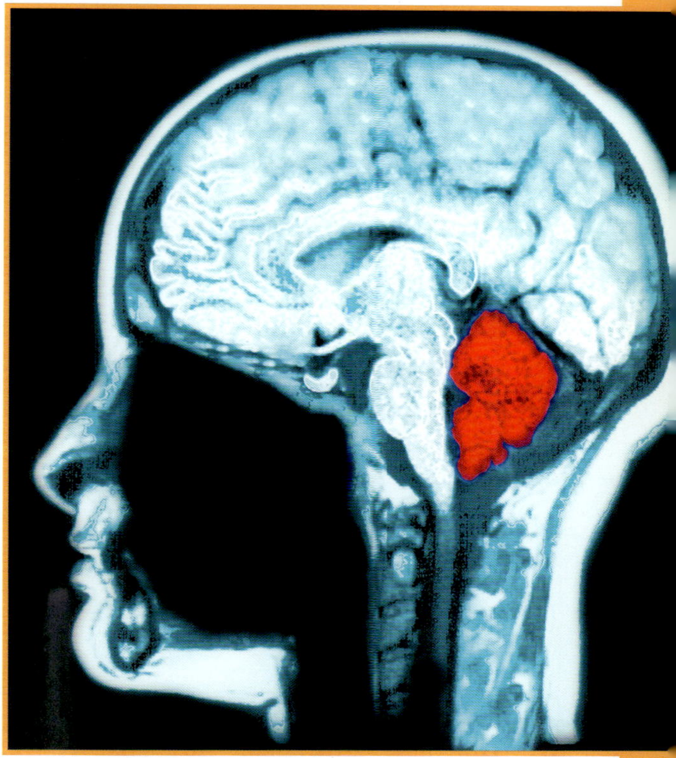

An MRI scan of a brain can show areas that are active in real time. It also shows how the brain reacts to stimuli.

TYPES OF LIFE SCIENCE

There are different specializations in life science. **This chart lists some of the most common areas of study.**	**Anatomy** The structure of animals and plants	**Botany** Plants and their life cycles	**Cell Biology** The cells of living organisms	**Ecology** Living organisms and their environment
Evolutionary Biology The study of how species have changed over time	**Genetics** Genes and heredity	**Microbiology** Microscopic organisms and their interactions	**Toxicology** Chemicals and how they affect other living things	**Zoology** The animal kingdom

Modern Astronomy

Astronomy was one of the earliest areas of science in which humans made accurate observations. In the modern world, astronomy has provided scientists with answers to some of the most challenging questions about the universe. The vast distances and huge time frames involved in space were first revealed in the 1920s, when the U.S. astronomer Edwin Hubble recognized that there were many **galaxies** in the universe besides the Milky Way.

Galaxies are groups of millions, sometimes even trillions, of stars. Many galaxies are spiral in shape. The nearest galaxy to the Milky Way, where Earth is situated, is the Andromeda Galaxy. Andromeda is larger than the Milky Way.

The English cosmologist and physicist, Stephen Hawking, developed a theory that all matter and time itself had begun as a **big bang**. This theory was based on the fact that galaxies are moving away from each other at astonishing speeds. Although the big bang theory was debated in the mid-twentieth century, Hawking's theory is now widely accepted as being true by most astronomers.

Theories about the structure and nature of the universe are increasingly complex. It is estimated that about 85 percent of the matter in the universe is **dark matter**, which cannot be observed using existing technology. There are also areas such as black holes in space, from which nothing, not even light, can escape. This is because black holes have an enormously strong gravitational pull.

While theories about the structure and future of the universe are difficult to comprehend, human space travel has become a reality. Space-station and spacecraft technology have made it possible for humans to visit the Moon. Space probes have been sent out through the solar system, satellites circuit Earth, and there are preparations for a crewed flight to the planet Mars.

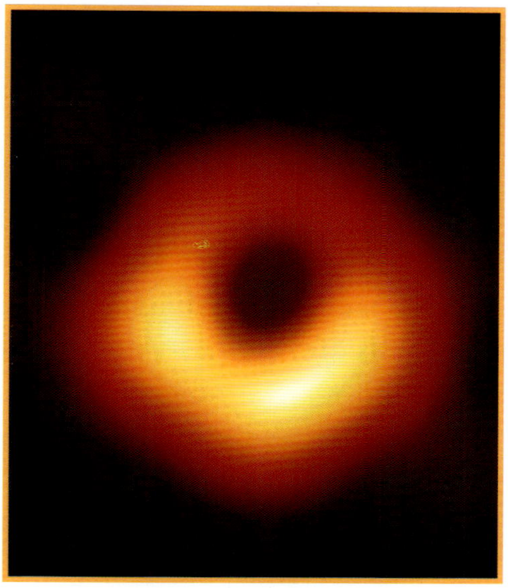

In 2019, scientist Katie Bouman worked out a way of taking a photograph of a black hole in space. She did this by programming telescopes located in different parts of the world.

The Andromeda Galaxy is
1.5 million miles
(2.5 million km) from Earth.

The Milky Way contains
10,000,000,000,000
different stars.

The universe was created
13.79 billion
years ago.

TIMELINE OF SCIENCE

It is not known exactly who or when the first humans started trying to understand the world. It is known, however, that people in the ancient world were carrying out experiments thousands of years ago. From about the third century BC, Greek researchers wrote down the results of their experiments. Knowledge has steadily increased since then. Many brilliant minds have made significant discoveries that have helped to shape today's world.

3300 BC	500 AD	1000	1550	1600

340 BC
Greek philosopher Aristotle describes the natural world and defines physics and life science.

3300 BC
Humans learn to combine copper with tin to make bronze tools. The bronze tools are much harder than copper or tin alone.

1543
Nicolaus Copernicus explains that Earth orbits the Sun, overturning centuries of beliefs.

1000
Islamic scientist Al-Haytham describes how light works. He develops ideas on how experiments should be carried out.

1687
Isaac Newton publishes *Philosophiæ Naturalis Principia Mathematica*, normally referred to as *Principia*, three volumes that describe the laws of motion.

1700 | 1800 | 1900 | 2000 | 2019

1778
French scientist Antoine Lavoisier discovers a gas and names it oxygen.

1859
Charles Darwin publishes *On the Origin of Species*, which describes a theory of evolution.

1916
Albert Einstein publishes his theory of general relativity, which explains how not only space but also time can be curved.

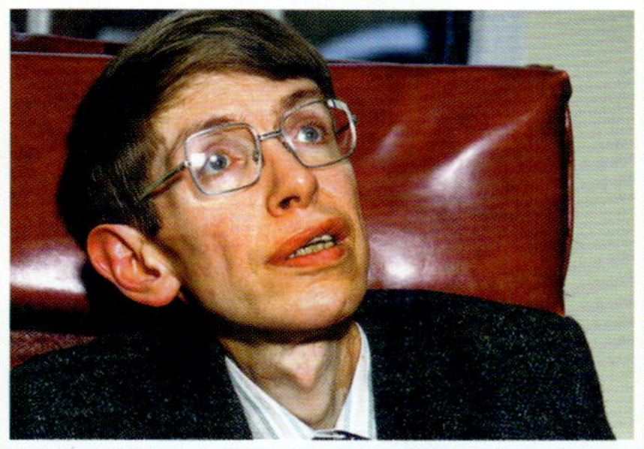

1970
Stephen Hawking and Roger Penrose publish their proof of the big bang theory on the origins of the universe.

2012
Scientists using the Large Hadron Collider at CERN in Switzerland prove the existence of the Higgs Boson, which is the smallest possible particle of matter.

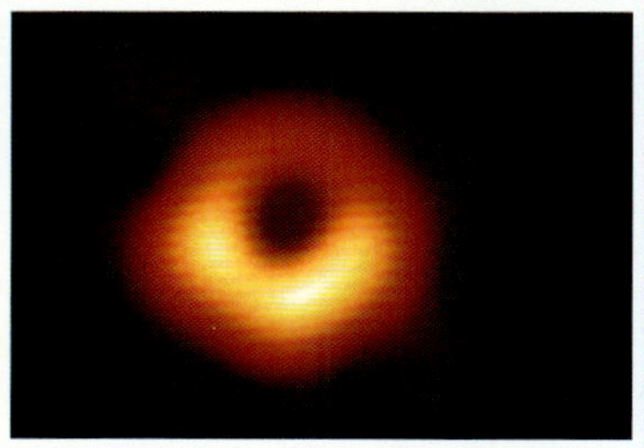

2019
Katie Bouman's calculations are used to take the first picture of a black hole in space.

QUIZ

ONE
What does the Latin word *Scientia* mean?

TWO
Which two elements form the compound bronze?

THREE
What did Aristotle think were the four basic elements?

FOUR
Which British thinker invented the scientific method?

FIVE
What is the speed of light?

SIX
What did Dimitri Mendeleev devise?

SEVEN
What do organic chemists study?

EIGHT
What was the name of Charles Darwin's theory of how life forms changed?

NINE
What do botanists study?

TEN
What is the name of the nearest galaxy to the Milky Way?

ANSWERS
ONE Knowledge **TWO** Copper and tin **THREE** Earth, air, fire, and water **FOUR** Francis Bacon **FIVE** 186,282 miles (299,792 km) per second **SIX** The periodic table of the elements **SEVEN** The reaction of other elements with carbon **EIGHT** The theory of evolution **NINE** Plants **TEN** Andromeda

KEY WORDS

alchemists: medieval scientists who tried to make gold from other metals

atomic theory: the belief that all matter is composed of small, invisible particles

atomic weights: the relationship of atoms of an element to the element carbon 12

atoms: the basic building blocks of matter

big bang: the moment when the universe came into being with huge force

biology: the study of living things

chemical notation: a way of using letters and numbers to describe elements

chemistry: the study of substances and their actions

dark matter: matter in the universe that cannot be seen

electromagnetic radiation: the spectrum of electricity, magnetism and light

elements: the basic substances in the universe

galaxies: groupings of millions of stars

genes: sections of DNA that pass on characteristics from the parent organism

geology: the study of what Earth is made from

laws: in science, statements that predict what will happen

matter: a substance that everything physical is made from

meteorology: the study of the weather

oceanography: the study of the oceans

periodic table: a way of arranging all the elements into a single reference chart

physics: the study of forces acting in the universe

radiation: the release of energy, especially the way that elements break down over time and give off harmful energy

scientific method: the way of increasing scientific knowledge by observation and experimentation

INDEX

LIGHTBOX

SUPPLEMENTARY RESOURCES

Click on the plus icon found in the bottom left corner of each spread to open additional teacher resources.

- Download and print the book's quizzes and activities
- Access curriculum correlations
- Explore additional web applications that enhance the Lightbox experience

LIGHTBOX DIGITAL TITLES

Packed full of integrated media

VIDEOS

INTERACTIVE MAPS

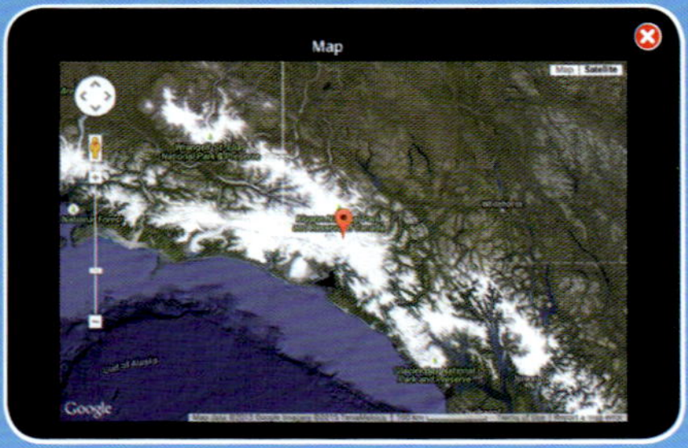

WEBLINKS

SLIDESHOWS

QUIZZES

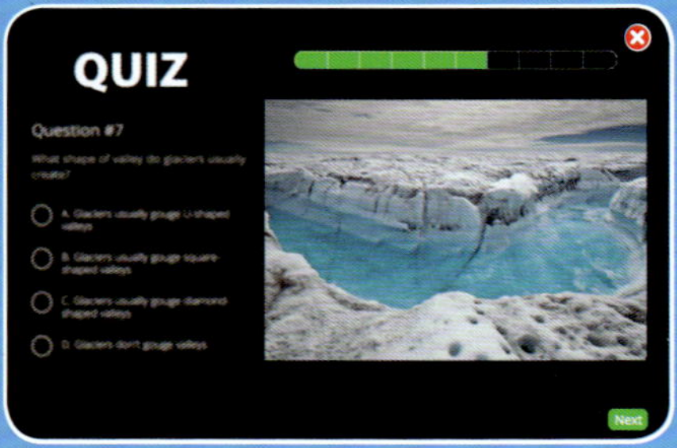

OPTIMIZED FOR

- ✓ TABLETS
- ✓ WHITEBOARDS
- ✓ COMPUTERS
- ✓ AND MUCH MORE!

Published by Smartbook Media Inc.
350 5th Avenue, 59th Floor New York, NY 10118
Website: www.openlightbox.com

Project Coordinator: Heather Kissock
Art Director: Terry Paulhus

Library of Congress Control Number: 2019942196

ISBN 978-1-5105-4410-9 (hardcover)
ISBN 978-1-5105-4411-6 (multi-user eBook)

Printed in Guangzhou, China
1 2 3 4 5 6 7 8 9 0 23 22 21 20 19

072019
121819

Photo Credits
Every reasonable effort has been made to trace ownership and to obtain permission to reprint copyright material. The publisher would be pleased to have any errors or omissions brought to its attention so that they may be corrected in subsequent printings.

The publisher acknowledges Getty Images, Alamy, iStock, and Shutterstock as its primary image suppliers for this title.